Original title:
Purpose: Not Available in Stores

Copyright © 2025 Creative Arts Management OÜ
All rights reserved.

Author: Nash Everly
ISBN HARDBACK: 978-1-80566-088-0
ISBN PAPERBACK: 978-1-80566-383-6

Silent Roars of Passion

In a world that sells it all,
My heart shouts out, yet feels so small.
I search for joy in every aisle,
But not a smile can change my style.

I tried to buy a little cheer,
But found a sock, not even near.
Wrapped in packaging so tight,
Where's the laughter in the night?

I took a chance, I took a leap,
Paid in pennies, counting cheap.
For moments gleam, but slip away,
Like sneaky cats at play all day.

So here I stand, in buyers' shame,
No golden ticket, yet I aim.
To find delight on shelves for none,
With silent roars, I still have fun!

The Unfolding Dilemma

To find a meaning, what a task,
Behind each label, questions bask.
I grab a bottle, read the hype,
But end up with a soap that's ripe.

A friend once said, 'Just take a guess!'
But guess what? I'm in a mess!
With guides and maps that lead astray,
I dance around like a cabaret.

In the quest for gold, I found a spoon,
Its shiny surface plays a tune.
As laughter echoes, I can see,
I purchased dreams, but not for me.

The conundrum twists, oh what a ride,
Can't buy a smile, can't store my pride.
Yet through the chaos, I still bloom,
With whimsy dancing in my room.

Footprints of the Unseen

I wander 'round where shadows creep,
In search of what can't be bought cheap.
With footprints left by dreams unmade,
I trip on thoughts that never fade.

A gaggle of hopes wave from afar,
Winking like a shooting star.
I step through cracks in time and space,
To find the laughs, to feel the grace.

In a corner shop where wishes live,
They say it's free—oh, what a give!
But as I reach, it slips away,
Like pudding pie on a windy day.

So here I stand, with dreams in hand,
No price tag worn, just joy so grand.
With every step, the fun runs free,
In footloose tales, just let it be!

Mysteries of the Unbranded

Why do socks always lose their mate?
They're on a quest, just wait and see,
To find the laughter in a sock's fate,
Hidden treasures, wild and free.

In a drawer, they plot and scheme,
To start a revolution, no tag in sight.
Forget the labels, let's just dream,
Who knew laundry could bring such delight?

Look, there goes a button, rogue and bold,
Forming alliances with lint, just right.
Together they make a story retold,
Fabric friendships, weaving the night.

So next time you find a lone sock's grin,
Consider the journey they've made so far.
Not all adventures fit neatly within,
Some just need a little bizarre.

Shards of the Unmarketed

In the cupboard, cookies plotted away,
The ones that never made the box,
Baking joy in a secret ballet,
While crunching sounds like little mocks.

Fate sealed them with a twist of fate,
No branding bling to shine so bright.
They dreamt of glory, to elevate,
But crumbs, they knew, would take flight.

Each piece a promise, a tasty trick,
Cocoa dreams and a sprinkle of fun.
In stealthy jars, they play their pick,
No store-bought rules when they're on the run.

So munch on these legends, bite by bite,
Unmarked, unfamed, but oh so sweet.
In hidden realms, find pure delight,
In shards of joy, life's little treat.

Oracles of the Heart

In a garden of whispers and shades,
A dandelion spoke with flair,
"I don't need a label, or parades,
I just blow dreams into the air."

The sunflower nodded, tall, proud, and bright,
"Who needs a brand to shine like the sun?
Authentic blooms in the morning light,
We're all here just to have some fun!"

Trees in the breeze swayed with delight,
Each branch a secret, each leaf a plan,
Growing and changing, out of plain sight,
Nature's way isn't for any man.

So listen closely, to nature's own tune,
In unmarked trails, the heart finds its start.
Beneath the bright day, beneath the moon,
The true oracles whisper from the heart.

The Shade of Aspiration

In a forest of dreams, tall and wide,
A shadow looms with a chuckle and grin,
"Oh dear wanderer, come take a ride,
Forget the labels, they're wearing thin."

With every step, the trees clap their hands,
Unmarked paths twist and twirl with cheer,
A dance through life's glorious strands,
Together, let go of all that you fear.

Each leaf, a lesson, a story untold,
The sun plays tricks, a tricky buffoon,
Chasing the rays, be brave, be bold,
In the shade of aspiration, find your tune.

So if you stumble on this merry way,
Remember the fun, let joy impart,
In crafting the journey, come what may,
It's all about wandering, not playing the part.

Stars Beyond the Price Tags

In a world of shiny things,
Where cash rules day and night,
I sought for brightness bling-bling,
But stumbled on a quirky kite.

Its tail was full of candy dreams,
With laughter like a bouncing ball,
For value isn't just in schemes,
It's found when we let giggles call.

The price tag waved, it knew the game,
But joy, dear friend, has no such score.
I flew that kite, and felt the same,
As if I'd won a giant store.

So take a breath, let fun ignite,
In every twist and funny turn.
Life's wonders outshine any price,
In laughter, watch the spirit burn.

Radiance of the Unmeasured

I walked into a shop of dreams,
Where gadgets go to sing and dance,
But what I found were giggle beams,
   That sparkled like a silly prance.

A clock that ticked with silly tunes,
And chairs that giggled when you sat,
These treasures held the charm of moons,
   And cost me naught but silly chat.

I learned that life can't be confined,
To tags or price that make it real,
It's found in laughter, sweetly blind,
   A treasure map, without a seal.

So search not for what's on display,
Dive deep into the joyous sea,
For unmeasured light will lead the way,
Where smiles and laughter set you free.

Beneath the Surface of Things

Beneath the waves of shiny goods,
There lies a world of jolly jest,
Where rubber ducks wear pirate hoods,
And laughter's always at its best.

I bought a mug that cracked a joke,
With coffee beans that danced around,
In everything, a secret spoke,
Of joy that can't be lost or found.

The price was high for serious fare,
But silly hats could fit the score,
With every whim, I'd grow aware,
That fun is richer than a store.

So peek beneath the shiny sheen,
Where giggles bump on tired knees,
You'll find the gold in what I mean,
Life's treasure chest is full of keys.

The Treasure Map of Life

X marks the spot where laughter begins,
A map that's drawn in doodled lines,
With valleys deep where silliness spins,
And mountains high with cheese and vines.

Each twist and turn brings out a smile,
With every "Aha!" a surprise,
Forget the clock and measure a mile,
In tickles found beneath the skies.

The compass spins on playful hearts,
Leading us to delight unknown,
Through silly games and funny arts,
Where treasure's claimed by laughter grown.

So take my hand, let's roam the map,
In joy, we'll never lose our way,
For every giggle forms a gap,
Where life's true loot is bright as day.

The Essence of Existence

In a world full of gadgets and toys,
They sell batteries, but not true joys.
Seeking meaning in cereal boxes,
While the cat just grooms itself and socks us.

We chase rainbows with laundry detergent,
Finding answers in fruit's ferment.
Look, a unicorn! Oh, wait, it's a goat,
Selling dreams wrapped in a cheap coat.

A sign that promises happiness free,
But all it brings is a bumblebee.
Our purpose lost in a game of charades,
Laughing at life's absurd escapades.

So sip your coffee, with whipped cream on top,
Dance like nobody cares if you flop.
For joy is a dance that's silly and bold,
Not found on a shelf, nor sold nor controlled.

Unraveled Threads

A life is just yarn, tangled and tied,
Yet here I am, with mismatched pride.
I knit a sweater but lost the ball,
Now it fits my dog; what a comical fall!

Socks disappear in the laundry's charm,
I swear the dryer holds a secret arm.
Searching for purpose in lost and found,
Only to see my sense of humor crowned.

Pull at the string, unpredictably wild,
Like a toddler's tantrum or an unruly child.
We wear our quirks as a badge of honor,
While the universe chuckles; oh, what a goner!

Let's weave a tapestry of laughter and cheer,
Finding fun in mischief, let's all volunteer.
So grab your thread, lay your fears to rest,
For being oneself is truly the best!

Treasures of the Soul

A treasure map scribbled on napkin neat,
Leads me to cookies—now that's a treat!
X marks the spot, but what have I found?
Just crumbs in my pocket—what's that sound?

I dig up gold but find just some cheese,
Aged like my hopes, yet still seems to please.
Buried riches in the backyard sand,
Turned into mud pies, now isn't it grand?

Under the stars by the grill we joke,
Life's deep meaning wrapped in smoke.
As laughter fills the night so bright,
Who needs riches when the fun ignites?

So here's to the rubies of laughter we seek,
Shimmering moments, not stoic or bleak.
For a heart full of giggles is worth more each day,
Than all the treasures heaped in dismay!

What Lies Beneath the Surface

In the depths of my couch, what will I find?
Lost socks and chocolate, my favorite kind.
Searching for meaning under the fluff,
Turns out it's just crumbs; I've got enough!

I ponder my life while staring at screens,
But deep down inside there's a dance of beans.
With every click, my purpose retreats,
Just a meme about cats and their endless feats.

My dreams lie beneath a pile of old books,
Along with stray pens and weird paper hooks.
So let's dive deep into this laughable mess,
And surface with joy; what a fun business!

For as I dig through the clutter of life,
I find silly moments that cut like a knife.
What lies beneath is not grave and profound,
But giggles and chuckles that spin all around!

Sculpting Existence Beyond Price Tags

With a chisel made of whimsy,
I carve my joy from the air.
No aisle to find this treasure,
It's crafted with laughter and flair.

In the store of bright ideals,
I gather what's free and sweet.
Discounts on life's little thrills,
Priceless moments, hard to beat.

Between the sale and the save,
I navigate my own delight.
No receipts for this adventure,
Just giggles in the moonlight.

So here I stand, a mad artist,
With colors fresh from the heart.
Creating dreams you can't buy,
In this quirky, vibrant art.

The Dance of Intent in the Silent Night

Under the veil of starlit skies,
I twirl with dreams, oh how I prance!
No flashy shoes or fancy ties,
Just whims dancing, a merry chance.

With each step on the midnight ground,
Intentions whisper, sly and neat.
In the silence, joy is found,
As I shuffle to my own beat.

The moonlight's a spotlight so bright,
A partner with no price to pay.
I twirl through thoughts in the night,
Finding laughter in the sway.

And though there's no audience here,
My heart sings loud in delight.
For the dance of the sincere,
Can't be sold, it's pure and right.

Raindrops of Passion on the Pavement of Life

When life pours down like rain,
Splashing puddles all around,
I dance like it's a sweet refrain,
My passions making laughter sound.

Each drop is an idea unfurling,
With splashes of colors bright and bold.
In the storm, my spirit's whirling,
Stories worth much more than gold.

I skip through streets, mischief-made,
With water shoes of carefree joy.
Splashing smiles, I won't evade,
Creating puddles to enjoy.

With every shimmery droplet's kiss,
Comes a spark that I can't replace.
For the essence of such bliss,
Is free and can't be found in haste.

Lanterns of Self-Discovery in the Dark

In a world that's dimly lit,
I carry lanterns full of dreams.
Every flicker, every wit,
Guides me through life's flashing beams.

With laughter as my trusty flame,
I wander paths both bold and bright.
No store can sell my claim to fame,
For my light shines out of sight.

Each twist and turn is part of me,
I dance with shadows, run and play.
Finding joy in mystery,
In the dark is where I sway.

So come join this merry search,
No aisles or tags will hold you down.
Together in this joyful lurch,
We'll discover joy, not the frown.

The Elusive Game of Existence

In the game of life, do we play right?
Searching for joy, like it's in plain sight.
Dodging the rules, what's the score, my friend?
Maybe the goalpost is just around the bend.

The coach is a cat, sleeping on the floor,
Gives tips with a yawn, 'Just ask for more.'
Referee's confused, holding up a sign,
Says, 'No one wins, just enjoy the wine.'

We chase after dreams like they're ice cream cones,
Only to find they're just melting drones.
Life's a circus, we're clowns on the run,
Juggling our hopes, pretending it's fun.

So let's laugh at the chaos, enjoy the jest,
In this silly game, we might just find rest.
Life's an elusive game, let's take off our shoes,
Dance like nobody cares, and choose our own blues.

Mosaics of Soul and Spirit

We're pieces of tile, all different hues,
Stuck on the wall, with eclectic views.
Searching for meaning in a jigsaw of fate,
Wondering quietly, 'Why must we wait?'

We'll stick to each other, like glue and old socks,
Create a mosaic, ignore ticking clocks.
A splash of wild colors, a dash of gray,
Who knew life's a canvas, and we're the array!

Chasing our shadows, they dance in the night,
Fighting with mirrors, they just won't sit tight.
Every small crack tells a story untold,
In the art of existence, we're all made of gold.

So let's mix our paints, and throw in some laughs,
Life's just a gallery, with mismatched paths.
A patchwork of moments, where laughter is free,
In this zany bazaar, let's simply be.

Navigating the Unmapped Life

Got my compass, but it's spinning around,
Lost in the fog, no map to be found.
Clouds are my guide, or maybe it's rain,
Whistling a tune, I find joy in the pain.

Every road I take is a mystery spree,
Whether I'm strolling or lost by a tree.
Squirrels my mentors, they scurry with ease,
In this uncharted journey, I might just freeze.

I hop on a whim, jump over the stream,
Who knew my route included a dream?
With each step I ponder, 'Where's that bright light?'
Heck, let's just wander till it feels right.

So here's to the paths that twist and they turn,
With laughter and snacks, for which we all yearn.
In this navigated chaos, let's relish the ride,
The mapless adventure is where fun abides.

The Sigil of Self in a Consumer World

Swiping right on life, what do I choose?
Labels and branding, but I'm feeling confused.
Retail therapy's just a temporary fix,
Like wearing a cloak made of thirty bucks' tricks.

In a world of ads that shout, 'Buy me now!'
I've lost my own voice, just don't know how.
Shopping for meaning in a mall full of style,
Perhaps I'll find wisdom in aisle number five.

I try on my dreams like a coat from a rack,
But oh, how it pinches, can't seem to relax.
Consumers of quirks, we gather and stall,
Trading our stories in this grand shopping mall.

So let's cut the tags, and step out the door,
Forge our own sigils, let our hearts roar.
In this hoarding of moments, let's cherish the jest,
In a world so consuming, we'll just be our best.

Filters of the Soul

A coffee cup full of dreams,
With sprinkles of laughter and beans.
Yet here I sit, with a mug in hand,
Trying to brew up a grand life plan.

My filter's clogged with socks and clothes,
I wonder if my heart still knows.
What's on sale at the thrift store today?
A cosmic joke? Oh, hip hip hooray!

The stars are bright, but my vision's blurred,
Found my calling, but it slurred.
I'll sift through the nonsense to find my jam,
Is a taco my goal? It surely can!

With giggles and hiccups, I chase the sun,
Life's more fun when you just run.
So I'll dance in the rain, remind you to smile,
Filters or not, I'm home, that's my style.

The Voice of the Unexpressed

There's a voice in my head that loves to hum,
Singing sweet nothings, making me glum.
Every time it speaks, I just roll my eyes,
It's like talking to a cat, full of surprise!

It whispers sweet nothings, taking a toll,
On my sanity, yet feels like a stroll.
What if I let it out for a twirl?
Would it dance in the air like a dizzying swirl?

It's grumpy and chatty, a hilarious blend,
Full of bad puns that just never end.
So I giggle and nod, as I try to confide,
In the voice of the unexpressed, let's take a ride.

Today's punchline might just be this:
Embrace the chaos, it's pure comedy bliss.
With laughter as armor, I boldly reflect,
Really, it's a joy to be blissfully wrecked!

Myriad of Paths

Life's a noodle, twisted and bent,
With choices like candy, which one's heaven-sent?
I'll follow a rabbit, then chase a frog,
As confusing as cats who just won't log.

A fork in the road? Bring on the pie,
With flavors so wild, I might just fly.
Should I bake cookies or join a parade?
Maybe both! Oh, decisions are made!

In a swirl of giggles, I'll skip down a way,
Where jellybeans bicker and gumdrops play.
Each path's a riddle, wrapped in a joke,
I'll dance through the choices; how could I choke?

For every wrong turn, there's a silly dance,
The map is a whimsy, a probabilistic chance.
So let's juggle our dreams, without a care,
In this labyrinth of fun, I'll always dare!

The Untold Story

Once upon a giggle, in lands far and wide,
Lived a chicken who wanted to be a ride.
Clucking like mad, it thought, 'What a dream!'
Hop on my back, oh let's go scream!

The cow joined the party, with mooing delight,
"Why can't we take llamas on our flight?"
They plotted and planned, with much to unfold,
A circus of animals, so bold and uncontrolled.

In a twist of absurdity, they wrote a tale,
Of feathered astronauts and cows without fail.
"Let's conquer the moon, with a bounce and a hop!"
Only to discover, it's just a lollipop!

Now that's the story no one had cried,
It's the joyous chaos we often hide.
So laugh at the llamas, embrace every plot,
And remember—it's funny, and that's what we've got!

Muted Echoes of Desire

In the corner lies a dream,
Wrapped in bubble wrap, it seems.
I check online for reviews,
But all I find are mismatched shoes.

I ordered hope, but got a cat,
Said it could dance, imagine that!
It prances 'round, a fuzzy clown,
While my ambitions tumble down.

Oh, the mantra of my plight,
Each laugh echoes through the night.
A cosmic joke, that's my vibe,
Spinning tales with every scribe.

If passion came with a price tag,
I'd buy it all, and dance my swag.
Yet here I stand with empty hands,
My vision lost in far-off lands.

The Weight of Aspirations

I lug my dreams in a backpack,
With granola bars, a water hack.
Each step I take feels like a chore,
But there's a donut shop next door.

I scribble plans on napkins worn,
Hoping to find the dreams reborn.
Yet every time I make a list,
I end up on a caffeine twist.

I wanted fame, a shining light,
Instead, I'm caught in laundry night.
The universe must find it funny,
As I trade my gold for old runny honey.

In this circus of high hopes,
I juggle tasks and miss the ropes.
Yet laughter flows when all has passed,
It's all a game, a quirky cast.

Notes on Ethereal Journeys

I packed my bags for a trip to bliss,
But all I found was morning mist.
Maps are drawn in crayon hues,
Leading to whimsical café queues.

I booked a flight to chase the sun,
Yet here I am, just barely run.
Each stop I make, a detour grand,
As ice cream trucks play in the band.

The stars above are winking bright,
But my compass points to late-night bites.
I follow trails of whispered cheer,
Where laughter blooms like wild frontier.

Though paths are lost in laughter's chase,
Mysteries unfold at a goofy pace.
I dance through dreams, a silly shoe,
In this journey of never quite true.

Unwritten Chronicles

My life's a book with pages bare,
Filled with scribbles and missing air.
I'll pen a tale of awkward glances,
In coffee shops that hold my chances.

Each chapter starts with coffee spills,
While mundane life gives me the thrills.
I wanted drama, love so sweet,
But found my plot in bakery treats.

Characters evolve in donut shops,
Where doughy tales never stop.
An epic quest for sprinkles bright,
Turns into night with a baking fright.

So here's to stories never told,
That fill our hearts with echoes bold.
In laughter's light, the tale begins,
With every twist, the fun now spins.

Crafted by Dreams

In a world where wishes roam,
Two left feet couldn't find a home.
With glitter and glue, I built a chair,
Hoping someday, it takes me somewhere.

Stars whispered softly, asking for tea,
While unicorns danced, just to tease me.
A rainbow slide made of jellybeans,
Is that a dream? Or just my scenes?

I stumbled through lands, all made of cake,
And caught my own tail, oh, what a mistake!
With laughter as bright as the sun does beam,
I found my joy, wrapped up in a dream.

So let's chase the giggles and sprinkle delight,
In this silly world, everything's bright.
With magic in pockets and a song in my heart,
Who needs a plan? Let's make silly art!

The Scent of Discovery

A whiff of adventure, oh what a tease,
Sprinkled with laughter, it floats on the breeze.
I searched high and low for a missing sock,
Instead found a map to a ticklish rock.

The trees giggled as I tripped on a root,
With each clumsy step, I danced in my boot.
A squirrel challenged my moves with a wink,
"Come join my acorn party!" it said with a blink.

Through clouds of cotton candy I soared,
Where candy canes grew, and dreams were stored.
Each twist and turn brought a quirky surprise,
With each wobbly step, I learned to improvise.

So let's bottle the scents of life's sweetest grime,
Laugh like the animals; let's savor the time.
With every discovery, giggles and glee,
Where the scent of adventure sets all laughter free!

A Path Untraveled

On a winding road with a rubber duck crew,
We pondered the meaning of what to pursue.
With garlic bread signs and rainbows so grand,
This uncharted trail was simply unplanned.

Nonsense was our compass, leading the way,
With jelly as currency, we dared to play.
A llama appeared with a hat made of cheese,
"Join my parade, it's guaranteed to please!"

From puddles of pudding to mountains of fluff,
We danced through the chaos, never enough.
As giggles erupted from butterflies' wings,
Let's serenade laughter with the joy that it brings.

In the end, it's not where the road leads us near,
But the friends we collect, and the giggles we cheer.
So grab your strange hat, and don't look back,
Together we wander, down our own track!

Embracing the Unseen

I went on a quest with a sock as a guide,
Through landscapes of giggles, I tried to abide.
Invisibility cloaks of marshmallow fluff,
Every twist had me laughing, just silly enough.

With clouds made of cotton, I floated along,
Where the misheard lyrics played all the wrong songs.
A mustache-wearing cat claimed to be wise,
But snorted with glee at my baffled surprise.

Chasing the shadows of what might appear,
My heart grew lighter as laughter drew near.
In a world of absurd, the punchlines unwind,
Where joy is the secret that's hard to find.

So let's raise our mugs to the quirky and bright,
For it's in our odd corners, we find pure delight.
Embracing the unseen, let our spirits roam free,
In this wildly funny dance, come laugh along with me!

Beyond the Retail Aisle

In aisles of things that shine and beep,
A quest began, not for cheap.
With carts of dreams and flyers galore,
I searched for meaning, but found a chore.

Discounts on joy, the laughter is clear,
But where's the aisle for good ol' cheer?
I tried the gadgets, the books, the toys,
Yet nothing there could bring me poise.

The snacks were great, the drinks were cold,
But life's big secret couldn't be sold.
I left the store with fruit and bread,
Wondering where my heart was led.

So here I stand, outside the door,
No checkout line on this giant floor.
The finds I seek don't need a tag,
They're nestled deep—a bit of a lag.

Echoes of Ambition

In echoes loud, my dreams would call,
I chased them down, I climbed the wall.
With visions bright, I set my sights,
Yet found myself on sleepless nights.

Oh, goals once clear, now blurry scenes,
Of coffee spills and stolen dreams.
I thought I'd find a shiny prize,
But all I got were alibis.

Ambition danced in crazy ways,
Like disco nights and wild displays.
I tried a map, a guide to show,
But milestones came and fell like snow.

In laughter's wake, through trials I pounce,
Yet all I seek cannot be pronounced.
Perhaps the journey's fun and zest,
Is where I find my hardest test.

The Journey Within

A sign outside read 'Journey Inside',
So in I went, with hope as my guide.
But mirrors cracked and walls all bend,
Self-discovery can twist and bend.

I searched for answers in my own mind,
And found a maze of thoughts unkind.
With breadcrumbs scattered, I lost my way,
Chasing shadows of yesterday.

Each thought a riddle, a puzzle to solve,
In this brainy labyrinth, watch me evolve.
I packed a snack, a napkin too,
For I'd be here for quite a view.

With laughter now echoing off the walls,
I dance along, despite my falls.
In every spiral, I learn to grin,
The real jackpot was always within.

Found in the Shadows

In shadows deep where secrets lay,
I stumbled on a game to play.
With lights turned low and whispers soft,
I sought the truth that danced aloft.

Behind the couch, under the bed,
Mysteries wrapped in cobweb thread.
I chased the dust bunnies like dreams,
Searching for gold in moonlit beams.

I flipped the cushions, laughed out loud,
What treasures hide beneath the shroud?
Old receipts and forgotten snacks,
A fortune lost in cardboard stacks.

So here I sit, in playful strife,
Finding joy in the hidden life.
The truth can't be found on the shelf,
Sometimes it's best just to find yourself.

Unlocking the Vault of Aspirations

In a world of plastic dreams,
We search for treasures, or so it seems.
Looking for passion behind every door,
But the key's lost down on the grocery floor.

Hamsters on wheels, we spin and run,
Chasing the sun, oh, wasn't that fun?
With plans all drawn in crayon bright,
But we often forget, where's the exit light?

We'll auction off goals—buy one, get three,
But who needs a brochure, just grab it for free!
Goals on discount, with oversized tags,
We laughed so hard, we dropped our price tags.

So when you walk past the store's shiny floor,
Remember your dreams aren't locked anymore.
Just dig through the chaos, it's all quite absurd,
In laughter we find, it's the best gift unblurred.

Stars That Shine Without Tags

Stars come out, but without a price,
Twinkling freely, oh what a device!
No tags required to light up the night,
Just wish on a comet, it's a silly sight.

Dreams take flight, like kites in the breeze,
No buyer's remorse, just do as you please.
Navigating life, where no discounts apply,
We share a good giggle as the time flies by.

Far from the aisles, beneath cosmic schemes,
There's a cart filled with laughter and silly dreams.
Buy one for free, just sell with a grin,
No tags in the cosmos, let the fun begin!

So gather your stardust, come join in the cheer,
Life's not in stores, it's right here, my dear.
With joy as our currency, we trade smiles and jokes,
In a universe of freedom, we're all just some folks.

The Poetry of Untouched Potential

In the attic of dreams, dust bunnies reside,
Where potential is parked, and aspirations hide.
Old boxes of wishes, all gathering mold,
Yet some have said they are precious as gold.

Laughter bubbles up, like soap on a spree,
What if I told you, they're waiting for me?
They're nestled in laughter, beneath piles of clothes,
What treasures we find, in that laughter that glows.

So hear the call of that whimsical muse,
Dance with your shadows, let yourself choose.
For life's not a mall, but a wild open book,
With pages of nonsense in every nook.

And with a soft pen, we'll write down the fun,
In sketches of laughter, let's be the pun!
For the magic's in trying, oh don't be contrite,
In laughter we spark, and take off in flight!

Hues of Authenticity in a Mass Market

In a sea of sameness, paint splashes bright,
Color outside the lines—what a sheer delight!
They box us up, but we twist and we shout,
Let's throw out convention, and dance in a drought.

Canned laughter echoes, but we'll make our sound,
We'll waltz on the shelves, with joy all around.
Why fit in a mold, when we can create,
A canvas of chaos, it'll be first-rate.

So grab a crayon, and scribble away,
In hues of mischief, we'll laugh and we'll play.
Let's hang our art where no one can tell,
As we twirl through the market, in laughter we dwell.

Authenticity sparkles like glittering stars,
Not found in the aisles, but where wildness sparrs.
So open your heart, let creativity flow,
In the mass of the market, we each are the show!

The Beat of a Heart Unchained

A heart once bound, now skips a beat,
Dancing free on clumsy feet.
No labels here, just silly dreams,
Like ice cream cones with sprouting beans.

A purpose sought in trampoline leaps,
Bouncing high while laughter keeps.
With every jump, the truth unwinds,
A wild ride, no ties that bind.

Like socks unmatched, oh what a show,
The winding journey, where will it go?
A treasure hunt for things not planned,
In goofy moments, we take a stand.

So let's embrace the quirks of fate,
In chaos dance and never wait.
For in the laughter, we find our spark,
Hearts unleashed, igniting the dark.

Finding Meaning in the Unseen Cornerstone

Behind the wall, there's something grand,
Like searching for a lost rubber band.
A puzzling quest in the house of fate,
Where crumbs of wisdom await on a plate.

With each loose floorboard, a giggle bursts,
Unveiling secrets, as curiosity thrusts.
Banana peels lead to life's great truth,
Wrapped in laughter, essential in sooth.

It's like the cat wearing a silly hat,
Contemplating life's big jazz like a diplomat.
The laughter echoes, our quirky bond,
As we chase the wonders of a world beyond.

So let's tiptoe past the serious sign,
And juggle the jests of the grand divine.
For in the silliness, joy intertwines,
Finding the roots in absurd designs.

Whispers of Intent

Whispers float on a candy breeze,
With giggles hiding behind the trees.
Intentions wrapped in candy bars,
A treasure map leading to the stars.

In secret codes of chuckles and sighs,
The truths of life wear mismatched ties.
On merry-go-rounds, we spin and twirl,
Finding sparkles in a wobbly whirl.

A sneaky fox with a playful grin,
Unraveling knots with a swift little spin.
Twirling thoughts like a cotton candy swirl,
In the field of dreams, let creativity unfurl.

So let's embrace the whispers that cheer,
In gardens absurd, where fun pioneers.
Life's great riddle, a circus parade,
Each laugh a lantern that won't fade.

The Quest for Meaning

In a quest for more than just a snack,
I roam through life without a map.
With quirky signs and floating pies,
The answers wink from the silly skies.

Like searching for a sock in a busy laundry,
Meaning hides where things feel quite dandy.
In chocolate rivers and frothy streams,
The laughter flows where the fun redeems.

An awkward dance, a pirouette in the air,
With purpose tied to a fluffy chair.
The balloon animals giggle and bounce,
In the art of living, we quietly pronounce.

So let's misplace our worries on shelves,
And revel in games that amuse ourselves.
For in this nonsense, joy is revealed,
An unexpected harvest, a laugh-filled field.

Limelight of the Heart

In a world full of shiny things,
My heart's a quirky little sing.
With mismatched socks and silly shoes,
I'll dance around, chase away the blues.

Who needs a stage, a grand applause?
I'll waltz with joy, just because!
With laughter loud and giggles bright,
The limelight's where I feel just right.

So if you seek a grand debut,
Look for the one who's slightly askew.
For in this show, I'm the star,
Waving my arms, saying, "Here we are!"

Let hearts take flight like kites in air,
With candy dreams, a frolicking flair.
Join the fun, let's break the mold,
In this heart-limelight, we'll be bold!

Notes from an Inner Compass

My compass spins, it likes to play,
It points to fun, but not all day.
With giggles echoing in the breeze,
It charts a course that aims to please.

Oh, treasure maps of silly sights,
Marking coffee spills and pillow fights.
Directions vague, but never wrong,
Together we dance to life's silly song.

Forget the map, we'll draw our own,
In a world where laughter's grown.
With sticky notes that make no sense,
We'll find our way, no recompense.

Each wrong turn leads to joy anew,
Dream odd dreams, that's what we'll do.
In the quirkiness, we'll find our way,
With laughter guides us every day!

The Unmarked Road

There's a road that's never shown,
Where wildflowers laugh and giggle grown.
With mismatched signs and fences bent,
We wander, wondering where it went.

Each step is filled with happy chance,
A wobbly, cheerful little dance.
You'll find a squirrel who's out of tune,
We'll join its antics 'neath the moon.

With cookie crumbs and silly hats,
We'll share our tales with giggling cats.
The destination's just a jest,
To journey well is truly best.

So take my hand, and let's explore,
The unmarked road we both adore.
With hearts so light and spirits free,
We'll make the world a jubilee!

Secrets of the Heart

In the vault of silly dreams,
Lie secrets wrapped in giggle beams.
With whispers soft and winks that glow,
My heart's a treasure, you should know.

What lies beneath? Just silly schemes,
A world where nothing's what it seems.
With rubber ducks and jelly beans,
The laughter's loud, the joy's supreme.

Unlock the doors with giggly keys,
To find the fun among the trees.
These secrets sweet won't cost a dime,
They dance with joy in rhythm and rhyme.

So come along, let's share the part,
Of all the secrets in the heart.
In laughter's light, they come alive,
With silly dreams, we all can thrive!

In the Market of Hope

In the bazaar of dreams, I roam,
Searching for a map to call my own.
They sell all kinds of silly hats,
But none of them help with life's spats.

A vendor shouts of fortunes bright,
But I just want to find what's right.
I grab a jar of sparkly glee,
Hoping it's the answer for me.

A lady sells a dance with fate,
While I stand in line to contemplate.
Pies of joy? They look divine!
But will they make my stars align?

In this cheerful, bustling scene,
I chuckle at what might have been.
With every trinket that I spy,
I wonder, do the clouds fly high?

Unveiling the Hidden Tale

Behind a curtain, whispers hum,
A tale of why we sometimes numb.
A cat with glasses reads the scroll,
While I just search for silly coal.

They promise laughter in a bottle,
But I just seem to lose the throttle.
An owl in a suit gives advice,
But wow, his wit really costs a price!

Jumping jacks in aisle three,
What's this, a dance-off just for me?
I step right in, it's quite absurd,
Who needs a plot? Just spin and twirl!

I leave with tales of laughter bright,
Forget my worries, oh what a sight!
With every twist, I spin and sway,
Life's more fun when I'm in play!

Beyond the Transactions

In a shop where giggles reign,
And happiness is not for gain,
I trade my socks for a pot of cheer,
What a deal, it's crystal clear!

A seal in shades negotiates,
For rubber ducks with funny traits.
I nod and smile, what a fine trade,
His laughter echoes, I'm not afraid.

With each exchange, I lose more weight,
Not in pounds, but in self-hate.
I buy some bliss in cupcake form,
Who knew joy could keep me warm?

As I skip through these quirky stalls,
I leave behind my worried calls.
Each silly item, worth its weight,
Life's quirks bring joy, and that's my fate!

The Unending Journey

With a map that's made of cheese,
I wander through this land with ease.
A sign that reads, 'Lost? Just Pretend!'
I grin, for joy is around the bend.

I meet a frog who claims to fly,
But really, he just needs a pie.
We share some laughs and a slice of cake,
A journey without rules we make!

Through fields of giggles, step by step,
Each path leads to another prep.
A squirrel sells tiny dreams on sale,
I grab a handful, can't afford to fail!

As the sun sets upon our cheer,
We dance together, no more fear.
For in this wacky, joyful zone,
Every step feels like home sweet home!

Timeless Strivings

Chasing dreams that slip away,
Like socks lost in the dryer sway.
We seek the gold, it's really fun,
But end up with a rubber bun.

With every step, we leap and bound,
Wearing shoes that make no sound.
Like fish who dance on sandy shores,
Can't catch our breath, we drop our scores.

So here we tread in merry spin,
With twirls and laughs, we grace the din.
In endless quests, let giggles float,
With strivings wearing comical coats.

In life's grand joke, we grab the jest,
Finding joy in our silly quest.
Dear friends, let's laugh and play our role,
In this mad circus, we find our soul.

Where Light Meets Shadow

In the corner of the spotlight's glimmer,
A shadow dances, getting slimmer.
They raise a toast to what's obscured,
And giggle at the light, assured.

The sun hides jokes in beams so bright,
As shadows whisper, 'Oh, what a sight!'
As laughter brews from lines we trace,
With every twist, we find our place.

Where bright meets gloom, we laugh so loud,
Making mischief, carefree, proud.
The punchlines sprout where we can tread,
And light and dark share secrets bred.

So bring your quirks, your quirks in tow,
Let's frolic where the shadows glow.
With winks and giggles, let us play,
In this delightful, funny ballet.

The Dance of Abandon

In fields of grass, we leap and spin,
With carefree hearts, we laugh within.
The world a stage for wild delight,
As we dance like bats in the moonlight.

We twirl like leaves on autumn's breeze,
With whims and dreams that never freeze.
Our laughter echoes, a joyful sound,
In wiggly ways, all thoughts unbound.

With every step, our worries fade,
In this parade, no debt is paid.
We prance like puppies on sunny days,
Chasing after happiness in a daze.

So let's embrace the silly tune,
And shimmy under the bright full moon.
With abandon, joy takes us afar,
As we dance, we paint our own bizarre.

The Light in the Mist

Amidst the fog, we trip and sway,
In search of wisdom, come what may.
The silver lining hides in giggles,
A slapstick hunt for all our wiggles.

In misty trails, absurdities bloom,
We chase the light, avoid the gloom.
Like clumsy sprites, we wander free,
In search of laughs that make us glee.

With every twist, a joke concealed,
In shrouded laughs, our fate is sealed.
We dance to tunes of unseen grace,
With winks and grins, we find our place.

So let the fog embrace our quest,
With quirky hearts, we'll dance our best.
In the sweet chaos, we will find,
A light that tickles every mind.

Searching for the Unheld

In the aisles of dreams I roam,
With a shopping cart and no place like home.
I search for joy in sale tags bright,
But all I find is a frozen delight.

I ask the clerk for something grand,
She hands me a map to a far-off land.
I thought I'd find a treasure chest,
But only a sandwich stuck to my vest.

In a box labeled 'happiness,'
I found a sock, I must confess.
The label read 'feelings inside,'
But all I got was a bumpy ride.

I left the store with empty hands,
Yet I chose to dance with life's demands.
I was searching high, and I was low,
Turns out, all I needed was a fun disco flow.

Remnants of Forgotten Yearnings

In a dusty drawer, I found a wish,
Wrapped in paper, like a great fish.
It swam through the years, bright and bold,
But now it's more stories than gold.

I tried to sell my faded dreams,
On a corner with hopeful screams.
But all they drew was a hungry crow,
Who squawked, 'Your dreams are way too slow!'

In a catalog of what could be,
Was a missing page labeled 'free!'
I flipped through chapters with frantic glee,
Only to find the "how" was a mystery.

So now I jot these thoughts down fast,
On napkins, torn maps, and broken glass.
For what's not sold is a treasure true,
A buffet of dreams still waiting for you.

Unsold Journeys

I bought a ticket to Anywhere Land,
And packed a suitcase, oh so grand.
But when I arrived at that shiny gate,
The sign said 'closed,' and I was late.

I saw a plane with one seat left,
But it laughed and flew off, so bereft.
All I had was my trusty backpack,
It whispered tales of things I lack.

I hitched a ride on a comet's tail,
But it was lost, oh such a fail!
We ended up in a cosmic mall,
Buying socks for space, who'd think that's all?

So here I sit with dreams to share,
Mapping routes to who-knows-where.
Sometimes, the fun is in the wait,
To find that journey where dreams don't sate.

The Canvas of Ambitions

With a paintbrush dipped in visions bright,
I swirled around to find delight.
On a canvas stretched with hopeful gleams,
I splashed my wild and wacky dreams.

I painted a tree that grew out of cheese,
And clouds made of marshmallows dancing with ease.
But when I sought to sell the art,
The gallery said, 'You're off the chart!'

I tried to frame a thought or two,
But all I got was a sticky glue.
My ricochet ideas bounced away,
I guess they didn't like to play.

So here I stand, my canvas bare,
With splatters of laughter hanging in the air.
For what I wanted was not on display,
Just a funny sketch of a brighter day.

The Quest for Inner Fulfillment

I tried to find it in a mall,
But all I found was a bouncing ball.
The sales clerk laughed and said, "Good luck!"
But I bought a set of funny socks!

I wandered through aisles, high and low,
With a shopping cart full of veggie dough.
I thought of purpose wrapped in twine,
Instead I filled my cart with wine!

Each gadget promised bliss untold,
But my heart needs more than items sold.
I left with shoes two sizes too small,
And a pair of crocs—please don't recall!

So I stand here with my shopping spree,
Hoping one day I'll find 'the key.'
Until then, I'll dance and jive,
In socks that make me feel alive!

Echoes of Intent in Silent Souls

I wrote a list of dreams so grand,
To find success with a gentle hand.
But when I checked that trusty note,
I realized I'd just jotted 'goto!'

I sought the sage on mystic hills,
He sold me candles and dreamy pills.
He said, "Find peace beneath the stars!"
But I got lost, and found a car!

In search of wisdom, I bought a map,
But it led me right into a trap.
I tripped on purpose-filled old cheese,
And laughed so hard, I dropped my keys!

So now I grin at every turn,
For life's too short to skip and spurn.
Perhaps intent wears silly shoes,
And lots of bows in vibrant hues!

Whispers of Destiny in Distant Skies

The stars above do wink and nod,
Yet here I am, still on the sod.
I asked the moon, "What's my fate?"
She said, "Dear friend, you're running late!"

The clouds conspire with silly grins,
While I keep plotting all my wins.
But every time I take a shot,
I end up stuck in donut spots!

I chased a comet, thought I'd fly,
But landed on a pie, oh my!
The universe just rolls its eyes,
As I wear cake with all my tries!

So here's to stars that shine so bright,
Their whispers twisting through the night.
I'll dance with fate while wearing stripes,
In a world that loves all types!

The Uncharted Path of the Heart

I took a route less traveled by,
With snacks in hand and a big old pie.
Each step I took led to a quirk,
Like finding joy in dirty work!

Maps and charts can show the way,
But I'd rather laugh and play all day.
With muddy boots and a funky hat,
This journey's wild, and how about that?

I stumbled on a bridge of cheese,
And danced a jig with all the bees.
They buzzed, "Oh human, quite a sight,"
As I pranced along without a fright!

So let them claim that know-it-all,
But I'm the one who'll have a ball.
With chocolate dreams and wiggly art,
I'll find my way, a happy heart!

The Sketch of a Dream

In the realm where doodles play,
Sketching dreams in a funny way,
Oh, what a mess of scribbles around,
With laughter, lost, but joy is found.

Chasing clouds on a coffee cup,
Each swirl a thought, I giggle up,
Nonsense shapes dance in my head,
With crayons bright, I'll forge ahead.

Lines that wiggle, colors that churn,
A masterpiece? Nowhere to turn,
Just silly smirks and witty sights,
In this sketchbook of endless flights.

So grab a pen, let's sketch away,
In laughter's grip, we'll forever stay,
For dreams that tickle, laugh and gleam,
Are the best of all, in a silly dream.

Colors Beyond the Palette

A splash of jelly, a hint of cheese,
Colors pop like a sneeze,
With ketchup drizzles on a plate,
Who knew lunch could create such fate?

Colors burst from every bite,
A rainbow feast, a silly sight,
Painting dishes, who cares to dine?
When dining turns into a wild design!

Chairs are laughing, forks are bright,
Silly sauces take to flight,
Sloppy swirls, a feast we cheer,
Every meal's a canvas near.

So mix your shades and stack them high,
We'll paint the world and ask not why,
With every laugh and silly taste,
A palette rich, no drop to waste.

Symbols of Discovery

A treasure map drawn in crayon bold,
X marks the spot where stories unfold,
With arrows pointing nowhere in sight,
Adventure awaits in comedic delight!

A magnifying glass that's just for fun,
To spot the humor that's second to none,
Each tiny thing, a mountain tall,
Discovery's giggles will never fall.

For every clue is awash in cheer,
Hidden secrets we hold so dear,
Let's dance with puzzles, hop and skip,
Finding joy on this ludicrous trip.

So chart your course on this playful spree,
With symbols of laughter, wild and free,
Each jest we catch along the way,
Turns ordinary hours into a funny play.

The Portrait of Contentment

In my canvas chair, I strike a pose,
With eyebrows raised in a comical doze,
Painting smiles with a brush of glee,
My greatest work? Just let it be!

With snacks piled high as my muse,
Each munch and crunch, I can't refuse,
A masterpiece made of crumbles and crumbs,
Contentment reigns; oh, here it comes!

Putting on colors like a clown,
With frizzy hair and a goofy frown,
The artist's life, a funny charade,
In an abstract world where joy is made.

So raise a glass to the silly scenes,
Where laughter swirls, and life redeems,
In the portrait of contentment, find,
The joy of creating, hilariously inclined!

Charting the Unexplored

With maps that squiggle and squirm,
We hunt for treasures, strange and firm.
X marks the spot, or does it not?
Maybe it leads to a donut shop.

Lost in a world of whimsy dreams,
Where logic's tangled in silly schemes.
We chart our paths with wobbly pens,
Collecting giggles, making friends.

Giant rubber ducks float in the sky,
And lollipops grow ten feet high.
Adventure awaits, with a wink and a nod,
As we skip along, feeling quite odd.

Dreams Beyond the Inventory

Stuck in a warehouse filled with boxes,
We dream of beaches, sunny foxes.
"Out of stock!" the label says,
But we're busier planning fun-filled days.

Countless gadgets with no bee and no phone,
Yet our imaginations roll on its own.
A unicycle made of gummy bears,
Zooming past those mundane wares.

We paint the walls with rainbow hues,
Transforming aisles into joy-filled views.
With each inventory check so dull,
We're dancing through life, always full.

Notes in a Bottle

Messages bottled, oh what a sight,
Affectionate words from the thirsty night.
A hint of pickle, a dash of cheese,
Love notes swirling with giggles and wheeze.

We toss our thoughts to the briny deep,
Hoping that laughter is what they'll reap.
"Dear future self, don't eat the glue,"
A postcard warning from me to you.

Drifting along on the ocean breeze,
Sending our giggles with utmost ease.
Each bottle bobbing, a quirky surprise,
As dreams swim up to the sunny skies.

Fragments of the Invisible

In realms unseen and riddled with jest,
Fragments of nonsense arise from the quest.
A shadow dances, a whisper sings,
Unraveling giggles, oh, what joy it brings!

We chase the air filled with dragon dreams,
And unravel laughter in silly schemes.
Invisible socks have stolen our shoes,
While wiggly worms share gossip and news.

In laughter's embrace, we twirl and spin,
Surrounded by whimsies that live within.
For in the quiet, where shadows play,
The absurd becomes our guide each day.

Whispers from the Uncharted

In the depths of unmarked maps,
Frogs hold grand debates,
Discussing life's missing snacks,
And dodging the fate of plates.

With squirrels weaving nutty schemes,
And raccoons with lofty dreams,
Every critter seeks the prize,
A slice of fun in the skies.

Yet, somewhere a beaver's working hard,
Building walls with a side of lard,
Singing tunes that make no sense,
While life drifts on in suspense.

Now a wise old owl replies,
"Chasing joy is what's most wise!"
While chasing tails, they giggle along,
In a world where quirks belong.

The Symphony of the Unseen

A cat with dreams of rock 'n' roll,
Strums the strings of a sunny soul,
While dogs play drums with their paws,
In a band of furry laws.

The goldfish croons in bubble rhyme,
Timing best with the clock's chime,
Cacti sway to the genre's beat,
As laughter lingers, oh so sweet.

Each flower dances in the wind,
With petals twirling, none rescind,
Even ants join in the show,
Carrying crumbs like stars in tow.

Amidst the notes of laughter's cheer,
The unseen symphony draws near,
Where joy unfurls and life takes flight,
In this quirky, starry light.

The Untamed Muse

A muse so wild, with tangled hair,
Wanders through fields without a care,
Chasing clouds and dandelion dreams,
Her laughter's sweeter than ice cream.

With a leap and a jolly spin,
She leads the goats in a dance akin,
To the rhythm of the buzzing bees,
Nosing flowers with giggles and sneezes.

Every scribble becomes a song,
In a world where silly stays long,
Drawing rainbows across the skies,
As butterflies flutter by with sighs.

So let the untamed tales unfold,
With every giggle, bold and gold,
For life is a canvas, wide and strange,
Where the muse plays on, with whims to exchange.

Reflections of the Heart

In the mirror, a duck grins wide,
Waddling with unspoken pride,
Its flappy wings and wiggly feet,
In search of snacks, so nice to eat.

A cow in shades, strumming tunes,
In the field beneath the moons,
Mooing wisdom with a flair,
While all around, joys dance in air.

With a glint in every eye,
The squirrels plot, with seeds on high,
Matters of heart, a secret game,
Reflecting joys that spark the flame.

So gather round, and share the cheer,
In every laugh, the truth is clear,
Life's reflections bring smiles abound,
In crazy antics, joy is found.

In Search of the Unseen Compass

In the drawer of forgotten dreams,
Lost keys jingle, or so it seems.
With a map drawn in crayon bright,
I wander aimlessly, searching for light.

The GPS says, 'Turn left, go right,'
But my inner guide's in a comical plight.
I trip over socks, I shuffle through clutter,
Hoping one day my compass won't stutter.

Directions are silly, like rubber chicken,
Yet I laugh and send my fears a-kickin'.
On a journey to find what's all around,
Maybe the joy is lost but found.

Amid all the randomness, I may just find,
That laughter's the treasure, so sweet and kind.
With each step taken on this wild quest,
Who needs a compass? I'll just be blessed!

The Essence Beyond Aisles

In a store filled with shiny things,
I lose my way like lost pair of wings.
Aisles abound with products galore,
But the essence I seek isn't in the decor.

I check the shelf with glitter and gold,
Yet my laughter's the currency, so bold!
Shopping carts filled with packages ho-hum,
But inside each box, it feels rather dumb.

I tried the cereal promising dreams,
But it turns out, it's all just themed screams.
If happiness could be bought, I'd be rich,
But I'm still just here, with this weird little itch.

Beyond the aisles, in my own little mind,
Exist the treasures so perfectly designed.
Take my credit card, just leave me the fun,
For the real essence has already begun!

Dreams Unwrapped in Invisible Packages

I ordered some dreams through a strange magic site,
With a promise of wonders, oh what a delight!
Weeks went by with no shipment in sight,
Maybe they're lost in a cosmos of light?

Daydreams arrive, wrapped in a bow,
But unboxing my hopes makes the meter run slow.
I peek in the package—nothing there,
Just giggles and whispers of dreams laid bare.

Invisible treasures, can't see with the eye,
Yet in my heart's pantry, they're stacked to the sky.
So I throw my caution and plans to the breeze,
Twirling in circles, embracing the tease.

So here's to the dreams that take time to show,
Unwrapped and revealed in the fun of the flow.
Forget the tracking number, here's what I find:
The magic was always, just tickling my mind!

Threads of Meaning in a Worn Fabric

In my closet hangs a shirt with a tale,
Stained with laughter and a splash of ale.
Each thread woven with moments gone by,
It dances and twirls underneath the sky.

Socks with holes tell of misadventures,
And a scarf with snags? Oh, it's got some censures!
Yet in this fabric, cozy and threadbare,
Lies a humor that weaves beyond what's rare.

I patch up the memories, stitch every seam,
Their essence transcends what dry cleaning dreams.
With every pull, a giggle flies high,
Making my wardrobe a joyful supply.

So here's to the fabric that wears with delight,
In the seams lie the stories, whether wrong or right.
For in this old shirt, stained and frayed,
I find all the joys that never did fade!

The Light Beyond the Checkout

In aisles of dreams, we roam and chat,
Finding snacks that make us fat.
With each step, a giggle released,
Checkout lanes feel like a feast.

Cashiers roll their eyes, oh dear,
For every sale, there's laughter near.
A lost receipt, a forgotten toy,
Turns shopping into quirky joy.

Sale signs dance in neon glow,
Reflecting dreams we barely know.
With carts full of whims, we float,
Like ships at sea, or a cozy boat.

An impulse buy, a knockoff gnome,
Adventures lived far from home.
In this market, life's a blast,
Who knew shopping could be such a laugh?

In the Library of Wishes

Whispers echo through ancient shelves,
Books giggle like mischievous elves.
A wish upon a page, we find,
For every story's a twist of mind.

Bookmarks flutter, dancing free,
Lost tales hidden, come read with me.
A dusty tome of love in the air,
Forget your troubles, just pull up a chair.

Stacks of dreams in chaotic piles,
Spilling secrets along with smiles.
Lost in fantasy, we float,
In this weird library, let's gloat.

The librarian smiles, a knowing look,
As we scribble our dreams in a nook.
Each wish we make, a story untold,
In this library, we'll never grow old.

Echoes from Unsung Realms

In realms unseen, laughter rings loud,
Echoing dreams amidst the crowd.
Unwritten tales hang in the air,
With jokes and jests that go nowhere.

Mismatched socks dance in the breeze,
As shadows play among the trees.
A dragon snores while ducks take flight,
In this wacky world of day and night.

Signposts pointing to 'nowhere fast',
Every moment a silly blast.
With fairy tales that spin and twirl,
Life's absurd in this strange swirl.

In echoes soft, we find delight,
As nonsensical dreams beckon light.
Let's run rampant through unseen gates,
For laughter's the secret that awaits!

The Thread of Uncertainty

In a world where plans are lost in more,
We laugh at life on an endless tour.
Stitching moments with a casual flair,
Finding joy in the unaware.

A tangled skein, a ball of yarn,
Wrapped in chaos, yet we can't be shorn.
With every knot, a tale unfurls,
Of misadventures and clumsy twirls.

We weave our hopes with threads of doubt,
In a dance of fate, we twist about.
A goofy grin when things go wrong,
In this sweet mess, we still belong.

So grab your needles, join the spree,
In this fabric of dreams, we're wild and free.
With each stitch, let laughter be cast,
In the quilt of life, we'll have a blast!

Markers of Significance in Life's Maze

In every twist, a marker found,
A left sock here, a lost hair crown.
Life's a map with silly signs,
Filling quests with quirky lines.

Where did I park my sense of glee?
Next to the snacks and that old TV.
With GPS that leads astray,
We wander on, come what may.

Mysteries hide in cereal boxes,
Unlocking thoughts like puzzling oxes.
Tickling brain cells, full of glee,
Fun is the key, just let it be!

So grab a snack and twist around,
Life's treasures lie in laughter's sound.
Markers of bliss, so small and sweet,
Guide us home, and can't be beat.

Shadows of Ambition

Chasing dreams on electric bikes,
Through shadowed streets, avoiding spikes.
Ambition wears such funny hats,
Like dancing cats and making chats.

Each step we take, a bounce and jig,
Like a pogo stick, a thrilling gig.
In the dark, we trip and slide,
Yet giggles echo, joy our guide.

Oh, what a sight, a cloudy quest,
With shadows cast, we jest and jest.
Tracing paths of grand esteem,
But real success is just a meme.

So laugh with me, let's not be shy,
Embrace the shadows, reach for the sky.
With each stumble, we laugh and shine,
In the end, our hearts entwine.

Light of Being

Underneath the disco ball,
We search for meaning, big and small.
Life's a dance with quirky flair,
Radiating light, we laugh and share.

From jelly beans to rainbow skies,
In every giggle, wisdom lies.
Our cosmic role, a funny script,
In the glow, we all are flipped.

With every wobble, twirl, and spin,
The light within is where we win.
Life's best features, odd and neat,
Are hidden gems beneath our feet.

So step into the neon glow,
Let your true self steal the show.
In this light, let laughter cling,
For joy's the best, oh, what a thing!

The Treasure of Unwritten Dreams

In a treasure chest with scribbles bold,
Lie dreams of pirates, tales untold.
Jot down wishes on crinkled pages,
Crappy coffee stains—the mark of sages.

The world's a stage with no rehearsal,
And dreams don't have a formal course.
Why not write with fruit-flavored pens?
Make a mess—who cares? The fun never ends!

From doodled hopes to wild ideas,
Every scribble laughs away our fears.
Lost socks, blank pages—what a team!
In the chaos lies our greatest dream.

So let your thoughts pour like a stream,
Unraveled treasures fuel the beam.
In every line that you've set free,
Lies the treasure of what could be.

Beyond Labels: A Journey Within

Labels stacked like cereal boxes,
With tiny toys that hold our flocks.
Beyond the tags, life's giggles float,
On rafts of whimsy, dreams we boat.

Who needs a label to feel alive?
Just of jellybeans, watch us thrive!
We crack the code of life's sweet fate,
Sailing dreams on plates of fate.

In every weirdness, a story gleams,
A journey unfolds through starlit dreams.
Forget the tags, embrace the thrill,
Life's about what makes us chill.

So ditch the tags, let laughter win,
Find joy with every quirky spin.
Beyond the labels, come what may,
Ride the wave, and laugh all day!

The Value of the Intangible

I searched for joy in aisles so wide,
But all I found was empty pride.
The laughter's cheap, the smiles on sale,
Yet genuine giggles seem to pale.

I tried to buy a sprinkle of fun,
But it slipped away, quick as a bun.
Their sales pitch promised bliss on loan,
Yet here I stand, quite all alone.

I tapped my card for happiness dear,
But the register squeaked, 'It's not here!'
So I laughed at myself, oh what a sight,
In store for a joy that felt just right.

If life's a shop, I'll set my own stock,
With puns and pranks, like a clown's tick-tock.
Buy nothing at all, let happiness sway,
The best things in life? They're just a play!

In Search of the Unpurchased

I wandered deep through shopping lanes,
Where everything's tagged with dollar chains.
I asked the clerk, 'Where's the giggle?'
He pointed to shelves, and I just did a wiggle.

I flipped through racks of wanted delight,
Found unwrapped funny, oh what a sight!
But everything glimmered, ready to choose,
Not the silly moments you can't peruse.

I pushed my cart through aisles galore,
Searching for items I couldn't ignore.
'Excuse me, good sir, where's the wit on sale?'
He handed me socks; I read the detail.

Next year's fashion? Oh, what a twist!
Nothing compares to the humor we missed.
So I'll shop at home for glee in my heart,
Where laughter and joy are a custom-made art!

The Hidden Compass

I bought a map to treasure unknown,
With X marking spots that shimmer and drone.
But when I arrived at the designated dare,
The treasure was laughter hung high in the air.

My compass spun in a charming mess,
Pointing to whims, pure silliness.
The directions were inside, easy to find,
In the heart of the jester, free and unconfined.

The road led to friends, no price on a smile,
We danced on the path and whirled for a while.
No GPS for joy, just a skip and a hop,
Where nuggets of giggles never do stop.

So follow your laughter, let whimsy steer,
In a world full of serious, set loose your cheer.
For maps lose their meaning when joy's in the chase,
And treasures lie fresh in the silliest space!

The Trail of the Uncommon

I took a hike down the path of the absurd,
Seeking the rare, where laughter's heard.
Each step a giggle, each rock a jest,
Uncommon humor, I found it was best.

Through bushes of puns, and trees of delight,
I found that the serious just couldn't take flight.
A squirrel in a hat, a dog with a tie,
All the oddities made time fly by.

The trail kept twisting, with chuckles galore,
With signs proclaiming, 'Just one more!'
But the best bit of wisdom took me by surprise,
That joy isn't bought; it's a priceless prize.

So here's to the journey, where laughter is lost,
No need for a price tag, just fun at all costs.
Each step on this path, with joy as my guide,
I found what I sought; it was always inside!

www.ingramcontent.com/pod-product-compliance
Lightning Source LLC
Chambersburg PA
CBHW051645160426
43209CB00004B/792